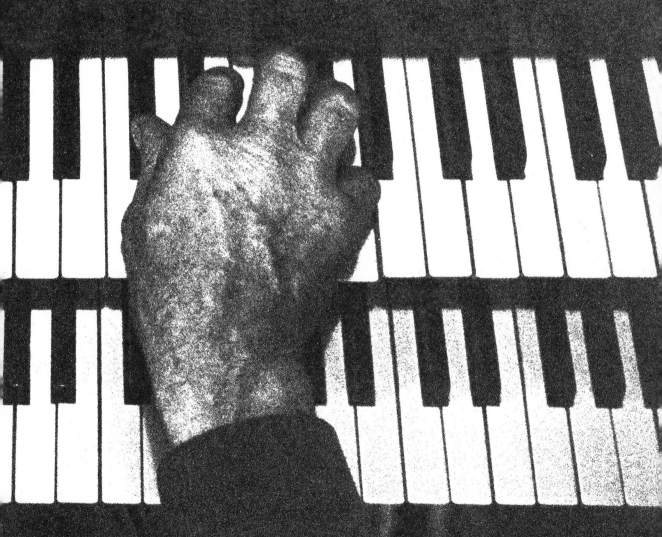

Stories of Our Favorite Hymns

Compiled By Christopher Idle

William B. Eerdmans Publishing Company
Grand Rapids, Michigan

First American edition published 1980 through special arrangement with Lion by Wm. B. Eerdmans Publishing Co., Grand Rapids, Michigan 49503

ISBN 0 8028 3535 X

Acknowledgements
Copyright hymns as follows: 'All creatures of our God and King', J. Curwen and Sons Ltd; 'Tell out, my soul', Timothy Dudley-Smith; 'Thank you for the world so sweet', Mrs Edith Rutter Leatham.
Scripture quotations are from the *Holy Bible, New International Version,* copyright New York International Bible Society, 1978.
Photographs: Barnaby's Picture Library, pages 8, 38 & 39, 47, 56 & 57, 64 & 65, 66, 69; Robin Bath, page 25; Jeremy Burgess, pages 41, 68, 71; John Cleare: Mountain Camera, pages 16 & 17; Colour Library International, page 49 and cover; Dover Publications Inc., pages 14, 33; Keith Ellis Collection, page 22; Mary Evans Picture Library, pages 10, 61; Fritz Fankhauser, page 42; Sonia Halliday Photographs: Sonia Halliday, page 50, Jane Taylor, page 29; Paul Kay, page 21; Lion Publishing: David Alexander, page 45, Jon Willcocks, pages 13, 20, 26, 28, 34, 46, 48 and endpapers; Ivor Philip, pages 54 & 55; Popperfoto, page 27; Anne Price, pages 30, 62; Jean-Luc Ray, pages 43, 60; RNAS Culdrose, page 35; Salvation Army, pages 58 & 59; Claire Schwob, pages 11, 18 & 19, 37, 67; Nabil Shehadi/Cedar Dance Theatre, page 36; E. A. Sollars, page 32; Swiss Tourist Board, page 9; Wales Tourist Board, pages 52 & 53.

Printed in Italy by New Interlitho S.P.A., Milan

Reprinted in the United States of America, September 1985

For as long as there have been Christians, there have been Christian hymns. Wherever the good news of Jesus Christ is heard, people start to sing about it.

When the faith began to spread in the ancient world, people wanted to know who these Christians were. The Roman governor Pliny wrote telling his emperor that they kept a strict moral code, met for fellowship meals, and on a regular day came together before sunrise to recite a hymn to Christ. Hymn-singing marked the Christian out: it could be dangerous!

For a different generation, television and radio have shown how much hymns are part of our popular culture, and how they speak to people's needs as much as ever.

Hymns express many feelings – joy and praise to God, love and concern, shame and penitence, hope and trust. They can often bring people together. Some hymns have been sung for centuries, linking us with previous generations. They can unite a vast cathedral congregation with lonely Christians in prison, a hospital patient with worshippers in church or chapel. Hymn-singing helps to show what a delightful mixture the Christian family is, with all its God-given variety of taste and temperament.

The English language does not have the oldest hymns, nor all the best ones. But it does have many of the most widely known and best-loved hymns. We have collected together some of them in this book. Sadly, we have had to omit some front-rank hymns and writers; but every one included is someone's favourite. We hope that many of them will be your favourites, too.

This book owes a great deal to the help of friends, librarians, my family and our church in Limehouse – the church most of all, because a hymn is not just words on a page. Hymns are meant for singing – they need people to bring them to life!

Although this is not the usual kind of hymn-book for congregations, I hope that as you read the words and linger over the pictures, you will want to join me in singing:

> *'Holy, holy, holy, Lord God of hosts, heaven and earth are full of thy glory; glory be to thee, O Lord most high.'*

CONTENTS

GIVE US THIS DAY OUR DAILY BREAD

AND FORGIVE US OUR TRESPASSES AS WE FORGIVE THOSE WHO TRESPASS AGAINST US

AND LEAD US NOT INTO TEMPTATION, BUT DELIVER US FROM EVIL

FOR THINE IS THE KINGDOM, THE POWER, AND THE GLORY, FOR EVER AND EVER, AMEN

OUR FATHER
WHO ART IN HEAVEN

ALL PEOPLE
THAT ON EARTH DO DWELL

The Swiss city of Geneva conjures up different images for different people. Some may remember holidays among lake and mountain scenery; others think of the United Nations and international diplomacy. It has also come to stand for the religious tradition of the Puritans, and the historic 'Geneva Bible'.

Even in the sixteenth century, Geneva was a great 'united nations' – of refugees fleeing from religious persecution. Among them was Scotsman William Kethe, who shared in translating the Bible and wrote this enduring hymn, based on Psalm 100. Its famous tune, written by a Frenchman, is known as the 'Old Hundredth'.

All people that on earth do dwell,
  Sing to the Lord with cheerful voice;
Him serve with fear, his praise forth tell,
  Come ye before him, and rejoice.

The Lord, ye know, is God indeed,
  Without our aid he did us make;
We are his folk, he doth us feed,
  And for his sheep he doth us take.

O enter then his gates with praise,
  Approach with joy his courts unto;
Praise, laud, and bless his name always,
  For it is seemly so to do.

For why? the Lord our God is good:
  His mercy is for ever sure;
His truth at all times firmly stood,
  And shall from age to age endure.

To Father, Son, and Holy Ghost,
  The God whom heaven and earth adore,
From men and from the angel-host
  Be praise and glory evermore.

William Kethe (d. 1594)

A tiny and remote country parish in Southern Ireland did not seem the ideal place for the brilliant young graduate to start his ministry – six feet tall with dark, curly hair, a classical scholar with great gifts as a speaker. But here in County Wexford, as a brash new curate, Henry Francis Lyte had an encounter which turned his ideas inside out.

A neighbouring clergyman was terminally ill. He confessed to Lyte that he had begun to re-examine his life as he read and studied the New Testament. He urged his younger friend to do what he had at last done: to stop relying on religious duties and good deeds for his peace with God, but trust completely in the mercy of Christ and his saving power.

This meeting immediately checked Lyte's contempt for the Methodists and 'enthusiasts' in the area. It gave him for the first time a truly personal faith. And it inspired him to write hymns such as this famous version of Psalm 103.

Praise, my soul, the King of heaven;
 To his feet thy tribute bring.
Ransomed, healed, restored, forgiven,
 Who like thee his praise should sing?
Praise him! Praise him!
Praise the everlasting King.

Praise him for his grace and favour
 To our fathers in distress;
Praise him still the same for ever,
 Slow to chide, and swift to bless.
Praise him! Praise him!
Glorious in his faithfulness.

Father-like, he tends and spares us;
 Well our feeble frame he knows;
In his hands he gently bears us,
 Rescues us from all our foes.
Praise him! Praise him!
Widely as his mercy flows.

Angels in the height, adore him;
 Ye behold him face to face;
Sun and moon, bow down before him;
 Dwellers all in time and space.
Praise him! Praise him!
Praise with us the God of grace.

Henry Francis Lyte (1793–1847)

Holy, Holy, Holy

'Dad, when was the first Trinity Sunday?'

Dad could not answer that perfectly serious and innocent question quite as easily as he could talk about the first Christmas or the first Easter.

Trinity Sunday is the one festival in the church's year marking not an event but a fact – the truth about the nature of God himself. And the words of 'Holy, holy, holy' stand almost alone among hymns; they simply attempt to describe, and worship, the three persons of the Godhead. Reginald Heber wrote them for one Trinity Sunday at his parish church in Shropshire.

When Heber was only forty, he became Bishop of Calcutta. But three years of travel and responsibility for the whole of India broke his health. Many of his stirring missionary hymns were published after his death.

Holy, Holy, Holy! Lord God Almighty!
 Early in the morning our song shall rise to thee;
Holy, Holy, Holy! Merciful and mighty!
 God in three Persons, blessed Trinity!

Holy, Holy, Holy! all the saints adore thee,
 Casting down their golden crowns around the glassy sea;
Cherubim and seraphim falling down before thee,
 Which wert, and art, and evermore shalt be.

Holy, Holy, Holy! though the darkness hide thee,
 Though the eye of sinful man thy glory may not see,
Only thou art holy, there is none beside thee
 Perfect in power, in love, and purity.

Holy, Holy, Holy! Lord God Almighty!
 All thy works shall praise thy name, in earth, and sky, and sea;
Holy, Holy, Holy! Merciful and mighty!
 God in three Persons, blessed Trinity!

Reginald Heber (1783–1826)

A violent storm at sea was the turning-point in John Newton's life.

Motherless at six and sent to sea on his eleventh birthday, he soon became a teenage rebel. He was press-ganged into the navy and flogged for desertion. Newton became involved with the African slave-trade and came close to starvation while living in extreme poverty in Sierra Leone.

But in March 1748, at the age of twenty-three, he was on board a cargo ship which was fighting for its life against heavy seas and rough weather. Worn out with pumping and almost frozen, he called out for God's mercy at the height of the storm, and was amazed to be saved from almost certain death.

Newton's life had many twists and turns. Eventually he renounced his involvement with slave-trading and, at thirty-nine, became a minister in the church. He persuaded the young William Wilberforce to stay in politics, and joined him in the fight to abolish the slave-trade.

Amazing grace! how sweet the sound
  That saved a wretch like me!
I once was lost, but now am found,
  Was blind, but now I see.

'Twas grace that taught my heart to fear,
  And grace my fears relieved;
How precious did that grace appear
  The hour I first believed!

The Lord has promised good to me,
  His word my hope secures;
He will my shield and portion be
  As long as life endures.

Through many dangers, toils, and snares
  I have already come;
'Tis grace that brought me safe thus far
  And grace will lead me home.

Yes, when this heart and flesh shall fail
  And mortal life shall cease
I shall possess within the veil
  A life of joy and peace.

John Newton (1725–1807)

Dear Lord and Father of Mankind

'I am really not a hymn writer', said the American poet who wrote these verses. And few who started to read *The Brewing of Soma* by John Greenleaf Whittier would guess what was coming. It is a long poem, describing at first how 'soma', an intoxicating drink, was made to prepare Indian worshippers for their frenzied Vedic rites. By way of contrast, at the end of the poem, Whittier turns to the God and Father of our Lord Jesus Christ.

Within twelve years of the poem's publication, these five verses were being used separately as a Christian hymn, and few now remember their origin. Whittier belonged to the Society of Friends, or Quakers, who, more than most Christian groups, have discovered the value of meditative silence in their worship of God.

Dear Lord and Father of mankind,
　Forgive our foolish ways!
Re-clothe us in our rightful mind,
In purer lives thy service find,
　In deeper reverence praise.

In simple trust like theirs who heard,
　Beside the Syrian sea,
The gracious calling of the Lord,
Let us, like them, without a word
　Rise up and follow thee.

O Sabbath rest by Galilee!
　O calm of hills above,
Where Jesus knelt to share with thee
The silence of eternity,
　Interpreted by love!

Drop thy still dews of quietness,
　Till all our strivings cease;
Take from our souls the strain and stress,
And let our ordered lives confess
　The beauty of thy peace.

Breathe through the heats of our desire
　Thy coolness and thy balm;
Let sense be dumb, let flesh retire;
Speak through the earthquake, wind, and fire,
　O still small voice of calm!

John Greenleaf Whittier (1807–92)

The chief writer of hymns for children in the nineteenth century was undoubtedly Mrs Cecil Frances Alexander, whose husband became primate of all Ireland. She wanted to help children understand the Christian faith. Of her 400 hymns, several were written to explain the meaning of phrases from the Apostles' Creed. 'All things bright and beautiful' explains in language children can understand the Creed's opening words: 'I believe in God, the Father Almighty, Maker of heaven and earth.'

All things bright and beautiful,
All creatures great and small,
All things wise and wonderful,
The Lord God made them all.

Each little flower that opens,
Each little bird that sings,
He made their glowing colours,
He made their tiny wings.

The purple-headed mountain,
The river running by,
The sunset, and the morning
That brightens up the sky.

The cold wind in the winter,
The pleasant summer sun,
The ripe fruits in the garden,
He made them every one.

The tall trees in the greenwood,
The meadows where we play,
The rushes by the water
We gather every day:

He gave us eyes to see them,
And lips that we might tell
How great is God Almighty
Who has made all things well.

Cecil Frances Alexander (1818–95)

Francis of Assisi was born into a wealthy Italian family. His father, a cloth merchant, was furious when Francis was converted to Jesus Christ and took seriously the words in the Gospels about giving to the poor.

Turning his back on a life of luxury, Francis travelled round the countryside with a few followers, preaching God's love for every living creature. He loved God's world of nature and saw all created things as objects of love which point to their Creator. And in the growing cities, he preached the gospel while living in utter poverty among ordinary people.

In the last year of his short life, ill, in pain and almost blind, Francis wrote his *Canticle of the Sun,* beginning 'All creatures of our God and King'. It was an early Italian version of the church's *Benedicite* – 'O all ye works of the Lord, bless ye the Lord'.

All creatures of our God and King,
Lift up your voice and with us sing
   Alleluia, Alleluia!
Thou burning sun with golden beam,
Thou silver moon with softer gleam:
O praise him, O praise him,
Alleluia, Alleluia, Alleluia!

Thou rushing wind that art so strong,
Ye clouds that sail in heaven along,
   O praise him, Alleluia!
Thou rising morn, in praise rejoice,
Ye lights of evening, find a voice:

Thou flowing water, pure and clear,
Make music for thy Lord to hear,
   Alleluia, Alleluia!
Thou fire so masterful and bright,
That givest man both warmth and light:

Dear mother earth, who day by day
Unfoldest blessings on our way,
   O praise him, Alleluia!
The flowers and fruits that in thee grow,
Let them his glory also show;

And all ye men of tender heart,
Forgiving others, take your part,
   O sing ye alleluia!
Ye who long pain and sorrow bear,
Praise God and on him cast your care;

And thou, most kind and gentle death,
Waiting to hush our latest breath,
   O praise him, Alleluia!
Thou leadest home the child of God,
And Christ our Lord the way hath trod;

Let all things their Creator bless,
And worship him in humbleness;
   O praise him, Alleluia!
Praise, praise the Father, praise the Son,
And praise the Spirit, Three in One;

Francis of Assisi (1182–1226)
translated by William Draper (1855–1933)

Hallowed
Be Thy Name

Let All The World
In Every Corner Sing

As a young man, George Herbert did not give much thought to God. But when he was thirty-six, he left the political rat-race of the court of King James I to become the rector of a country parish near Salisbury.

One of Herbert's great joys was music. Twice a week he would walk into Salisbury to play and sing with his friends at the cathedral.

One day he stopped on the way to help a man whose horse had collapsed in the mud under its load. The group of friends in Salisbury were surprised when Herbert, usually so smart and clean, arrived 'so soiled and discomposed'. One said he had 'disparaged himself by so dirty an employment'.

Herbert replied that the thought of what he had done would be music to him at midnight – and that the omission of it would have made discord in his conscience. 'I am bound to practise what I pray for...and I praise God for this occasion. Come, let's tune our instruments!'

Let all the world in every corner sing,
   My God and King!
   The heavens are not too high,
   His praise may thither fly;
   The earth is not too low,
   His praises there may grow.
Let all the world in every corner sing,
   My God and King!

Let all the world in every corner sing,
   My God and King!
   The church with psalms must shout,
   No door can keep them out;
   But above all, the heart
   Must bear the longest part.
Let all the world in every corner sing,
   My God and King!

George Herbert (1593–1632)

TELL OUT, MY SOUL, THE GREATNESS OF THE LORD

The seventeenth century was the great age of Bible translation. Parts of the eighteenth and nineteenth were boom periods for new hymns. The second half of the twentieth century has seen a flood of exciting new versions of the Bible in English as well as an upsurge of contemporary hymn-writing.

When Timothy Dudley-Smith was sent a review copy of the 1961 *New English Bible*, he was very struck by the beginning of Luke's Gospel. In this version, the *Magnificat,* or 'Song of Mary', begins with the words 'Tell out, my soul, the greatness of the Lord'. They inspired him to write this paraphrase, which is now one of the most popular of all modern hymns. It is the only hymn in our book by a living author, but it stands as a reminder that the tradition of writing and singing new Christian songs is alive and well.

Tell out, my soul, the greatness of the Lord!
Unnumbered blessings, give my spirit voice;
Tender to me the promise of his word;
In God my Saviour shall my heart rejoice.

Tell out, my soul, the greatness of his name!
Make known his might, the deeds his arm has done;
His mercy sure, from age to age the same;
His holy name – the Lord, the Mighty One.

Tell out, my soul, the greatness of his might!
Powers and dominions lay their glory by.
Proud hearts and stubborn wills are put to flight,
The hungry fed, the humble lifted high.

Tell out, my soul, the glories of his word!
Firm is his promise, and his mercy sure.
Tell out, my soul, the greatness of the Lord
To children's children and for evermore!

Timothy Dudley-Smith (b. 1926)

Fanny Crosby, the American singer and musician, was blind from the age of six weeks. She married her music teacher, Alexander Van Alstyne, who was also blind. She once signed an unusual contract with a publisher: to write three songs every week all through the year. In all she wrote many thousands.

Although American evangelists Moody and Sankey used this hymn on their missions, it did not become an immediate favourite. But Billy Graham featured it in his Harringay crusade in 1954 – and soon Londoners were singing it on their way home, in streets and bus queues and underground trains.

Dr Graham took it back to the United States, introduced it next at Nashville, Tennessee, and saw it take its place in the group of top favourites.

To God be the glory! great things he hath done!
So loved he the world that he gave us his Son,
Who yielded his life an atonement for sin,
And opened the life-gate that all may go in.

Praise the Lord! Praise the Lord! Let the earth hear
his voice!
Praise the Lord! Praise the Lord! Let the people rejoice!
O come to the Father through Jesus the Son;
And give him the glory – great things he hath done!

O perfect redemption, the purchase of blood!
To every believer the promise of God;
The vilest offender who truly believes,
That moment from Jesus a pardon receives.

Great things he hath taught us, great things he hath done,
And great our rejoicing through Jesus the Son:
But purer and higher and greater will be
Our wonder, our transport, when Jesus we see!

Fanny Crosby (1820–1915)

Germany in the seventeenth century was in the throes of the Thirty Years' War. Martin Rinkart was a Lutheran pastor in the walled city of Eilenberg in Saxony. In spite of his frail physique, he stayed there throughout the war, enduring the horrors of famine and plague. He helped refugees from other areas who came to the city. When all the other pastors had either fled or died, he ministered to the sick and dying, and conducted some 4,500 funerals, including that of his own wife.

Towards the end of the war, the city was besieged or overrun, once by the Austrians and twice by the Swedes. The Swedish general demanded a vast levy from Eilenberg's already desperate citizens; Martin pleaded with him, but in vain. So he turned to his friends and said, 'Come, my children; we can find no mercy with man – let us take refuge with God.' The general was so moved at seeing pastor and people praying and singing on their knees that the demand was reduced to less than a twentieth of the original sum.

This hymn, which began as a family grace said before meals, was sung as a national thanksgiving at the end of the Thirty Years' War.

Now thank we all our God
  With hearts and hands and voices,
Who wondrous things hath done,
  In whom his world rejoices;
Who from our mother's arms
  Hath blessed us on our way
With countless gifts of love,
  And still is ours today.

O may this bounteous God
  Through all our life be near us,
With ever joyful hearts
  And blessèd peace to cheer us;
And keep us in his grace,
  And guide us when perplexed,
And free us from all ills
  In this world and the next.

All praise and thanks to God
  The Father now be given,
The Son, and Holy Ghost,
  Supreme in highest heaven;
The one eternal God,
  Whom earth and heaven adore
For thus it was, is now,
  And shall be evermore.

Martin Rinkart (1586–1649)
translated by Catherine Winkworth (1827–78)

Neither John Newton's language nor his talent for verse had always been used for sacred purposes. In his early days on board ship, he taught the rest of the crew a song he had composed; what the lyrics said about the captain, his character, his family and his ship, was unprintable – like most of Newton's general conversation.

Another captain under whom he served was so appalled by Newton's constant blasphemy that when the weather turned stormy, he was convinced that he had a Jonah on board: Newton would have to go!

His conversion to Jesus Christ brought about startling changes for Newton, and this hymn is clear evidence that his mouth had had a spring-clean! He now used the name of Jesus in a new way, and his gift for choice words had been completely redirected.

How sweet the name of Jesus sounds
  In a believer's ear!
It soothes his sorrows, heals his wounds,
  And drives away his fear.

It makes the wounded spirit whole,
  And calms the troubled breast;
'Tis manna to the hungry soul,
  And to the weary rest.

Dear name! the rock on which I build,
  My shield and hiding-place,
My never-failing treasury filled
  With boundless stores of grace.

Jesus! my Shepherd, Husband, Friend.
  My Prophet, Priest, and King,
My Lord, my Life, my Way, my End,
  Accept the praise I bring.

Weak is the effort of my heart,
  And cold my warmest thought;
But when I see thee as thou art,
  I'll praise thee as I ought.

Till then I would thy love proclaim
  With every fleeting breath;
And may the music of thy name
  Refresh my soul in death.

John Newton (1725–1807)

Charles Wesley was never quite sure of his own birthday. It was, after all, just before Christmas; he was his mother's eighteenth child, born some weeks premature, so small and frail that he seemed more dead than alive. For two months he neither cried nor opened his eyes.

But he was quite sure of the date of what he called his 'second birth' – 21 May 1738. On that day he responded to the love and grace of God. He wrote this hymn a year later, 'For the anniversary day of one's conversion'.

O for a thousand tongues to sing
My great Redeemer's praise,
The glories of my God and King,
The triumphs of his grace!

Jesus! the name that charms our fears,
That bids our sorrows cease;
'Tis music in the sinner's ears,
'Tis life, and health, and peace.

He breaks the power of cancelled sin,
He sets the prisoner free;
His blood can make the foulest clean,
His blood availed for me.

He speaks, and, listening to his voice,
New life the dead receive,
The mournful, broken hearts rejoice,
The humble poor believe.

Hear him, ye deaf; his praise, ye dumb,
Your loosened tongues employ;
Ye blind, behold your Saviour come,
And leap, ye lame, for joy.

My gracious Master and my God,
Assist me to proclaim,
To spread through all the earth abroad
The honours of thy name.

Charles Wesley (1707–88)

Young William Ewart Gladstone, who later became British Prime Minister, greatly appreciated the services at Margaret Chapel in London's West End. For one thing, the sermons were short – never more than twenty minutes! More important, the congregation were 'the most devout and hearty that I have ever seen'.

The minister at that time was Frederick Oakeley – one of the leaders of the nineteenth-century Oxford Movement. He believed passionately in the power of ritual, religious symbols and fine music. And before he joined the Roman Catholic Church, he gave his congregation – and the world – this version of the eighteenth-century 'Adeste, fideles'.

O come, all ye faithful,
Joyful and triumphant,
O come ye, O come ye to Bethlehem;
Come and behold him,
Born the King of angels:
O come, let us adore him,
O come, let us adore him,
O come, let us adore him, Christ the Lord.

God of God,
Light of Light,
Lo! he abhors not the virgin's womb;
Very God,
Begotten not created:

Sing, choirs of angels,
Sing in exultation,
Sing, all ye citizens of heaven above,
'Glory to God
In the highest':

Yea, Lord, we greet thee,
Born this happy morning,
Jesu, to thee be glory given!
Word of the Father,
Now in flesh appearing:

Frederick Oakeley (1802–80)

THY KINGDOM COME

JOY TO THE WORLD!
THE LORD IS COME!

As the world's leading gospel singer prior to her death in 1972, Mahalia Jackson mixed with princesses and presidents, film-stars and top entertainers. But she turned down countless lucrative offers from bars, night-clubs and theatres – anywhere that liquor was sold. And she never sang the blues, considering it 'Devil's music'.

As a child in the poverty of New Orleans, Mahalia started singing. 'Hand me down my silver trumpet, Gabriel' was a life-long favourite, but so were the 'old Dr Watts' hymns of her Baptist church.

One Christmas, a blizzard stopped her going from Chicago to Memphis, where she was due to sing for civil rights workers in the negro college. So she called the telephone company, and from 8358 Indiana she held the 'phone for half an hour, and sang: 'Born in Bethlehem', 'Silent Night' and the 'old Dr Watts' – 'Joy to the World!'

Joy to the world! the Lord is come!
　Let earth receive her King!
Let every heart prepare him room,
　And heaven and nature sing.

Joy to the earth! the Saviour reigns!
　Let men their songs employ!
While fields and floods, rocks, hills, and plains
　Repeat the sounding joy.

No more let sins and sorrows grow,
　Nor thorns infest the ground;
He comes to make his blessings flow
　Far as the curse is found.

He rules the world with truth and grace,
　And makes the nations prove
The glories of his righteousness,
　And wonders of his love.

Isaac Watts (1674–1748)

On Whit Sunday 1862, some 5,000 people from the South Sea islands of Tonga, Fiji and Samoa gathered under the spreading branches of the banyan trees in the presence of their king.

Some were chiefs and warriors who until recently had been fighting bitter wars of cannibalism and revenge; with them were wives and families. That day marked their first meeting under a Christian constitution, with a Christian king, and in the knowledge of the Christian gospel.

This hymn, which had started life as a Hebrew psalm nearly 1,000 years before Christ, and was translated as a Christian hymn by Isaac Watts, opened the celebrations on that Sunday in the South Seas. It was a colourful and harmonious fulfilment of the prophecy contained in the words.

Jesus shall reign where'er the sun
Doth his successive journeys run;
His kingdom stretch from shore to shore
Till moons shall wax and wane no more.

For him shall endless prayer be made,
And praises throng to crown his head;
His name like sweet perfume shall rise
With every morning sacrifice.

People and realms of every tongue
Dwell on his love with sweetest song;
And infant voices shall proclaim
Their early blessings on his name.

Blessings abound where'er he reigns;
The prisoner leaps to lose his chains,
The weary find eternal rest,
And all the sons of want are blest.

Where he displays his healing power
Death and the curse are known no more;
In him the tribes of Adam boast
More blessings than their father lost.

Let every creature rise and bring
Peculiar honours to our King;
Angels descend with songs again,
And earth repeat the long Amen.

Isaac Watts (1674–1748)

And there were shepherds living out in the fields near by, keeping watch over their flocks at night. An angel of the Lord appeared to them, and the glory of the Lord shone around them, and they were terrified. But the angel said to them, 'Do not be afraid. I bring you good news of great joy that will be for all the people. Today in the town of David a Saviour has been born to you; he is Christ the Lord. This will be a sign to you: You will find a baby wrapped in strips of cloth and lying in a manger.'

Suddenly a great company of the heavenly host appeared with the angel, praising God and saying,

> 'Glory to God in the highest,
> and on earth peace to men
> on whom his favour rests.'
> *Luke 2:8-14*

Hark! the herald-angels sing
Glory to the new-born King,
Peace on earth, and mercy mild,
God and sinners reconciled.
Joyful, all ye nations, rise,
Join the triumph of the skies;
With the angelic host proclaim
'Christ is born in Bethlehem.'
Hark! the herald-angels sing
Glory to the new-born King.

Christ, by highest heaven adored,
Christ, the everlasting Lord,
Late in time behold him come,
Offspring of a virgin's womb.
Veiled in flesh the Godhead see!
Hail, the incarnate Deity!
Pleased as Man with man to dwell,
Jesus, our Emmanuel.

Hail, the heaven-born Prince of Peace!
Hail, the Sun of Righteousness!
Light and life to all he brings,
Risen with healing in his wings.
Mild he lays his glory by,
Born that man no more may die,
Born to raise the sons of earth,
Born to give them second birth.

Charles Wesley (1707–88) and others

Martin Luther King, near to exhaustion, was concluding an impromptu speech at Memphis, Tennessee, on 3 April 1968. This outstanding leader of the American Civil Rights movement, pledged to non-violence, was sharing with his hearers the vision of glory first glimpsed by hymn-writer Mrs Howe in the fight against slavery:

'I just want to do God's will. And He's allowed me to go up the mountain. And I've looked over, and I've seen the promised land. I may not get there with you, but I want you to know tonight that we as a people will get to the promised land.

'So I'm happy tonight, I'm not worried about anything. I'm not fearing any man. Mine eyes have seen the glory of the coming of the Lord!'

The next afternoon, as Dr King was chatting with friends on the balcony of the Lorraine Motel, he was shot by a hidden assassin. He died in hospital an hour later.

Mine eyes have seen the glory of the coming of the Lord;
He is trampling out the vintage where the grapes of wrath are stored;
He hath loosed the fateful lightning of his terrible swift sword:
　His Truth is marching on.

Glory, glory, hallelujah!
Glory, glory, hallelujah!
Glory, glory, hallelujah!
Our God is marching on.

He has sounded forth the trumpet that shall never call retreat;
He is sifting out the hearts of men before his judgment seat;
O be swift, my soul, to answer him; be jubilant, my feet!
　His Day is marching on.

In the beauty of the morning Christ was born across the sea,
With a glory in his bosom that transfigures you and me.
As he died to make men holy, let us live to make men free;
　For God is marching on.

Julia Ward Howe (1819–1910)

Thomas Kelly was the son of an Irish judge. He was ordained but fell foul of his bishop and founded his own sect, which eventually died with him. But this hymn has stood the test of time.

Kelly's practical faith was put to the test during a year of severe famine. He was loved by the poorest of the people for his kindness. One man cheered up his anxious wife by saying, 'Hold up, Bridget – there's always Mister Kelly to pull us out of the mire after we've sunk for the last time!'

The head that once was crowned with thorns
Is crowned with glory now:
A royal diadem adorns
The mighty Victor's brow.

The highest place that heaven affords
Is his, is his by right,
The King of kings and Lord of lords,
And heaven's eternal Light;

The joy of all who dwell above,
The joy of all below,
To whom he manifests his love,
And grants his name to know.

To them the cross, with all its shame,
With all its grace is given:
Their name an everlasting name,
Their joy the joy of heaven.

They suffer with their Lord below,
They reign with him above,
Their profit and their joy to know
The mystery of his love.

The cross he bore is life and health,
Though shame and death to him;
His people's hope, his people's wealth,
Their everlasting theme.

Thomas Kelly (1769–1855)

O COME, O COME, EMMANUEL

John Mason Neale was a born scholar. Before he was ten, he edited his own hand-written family magazine. As a shy but strong-minded young man, he could often be seen making a brass-rubbing or collecting architectural details in country churches he visited on his walking-tours.

He grew up to love the Middle Ages and the medieval church, the early church fathers and the lives of the saints. One small girl at his orphanage said that Mr Neale (then in his forties) 'must be very old, to have talked to so many saints and martyrs'.

This Advent hymn is from a Latin original of doubtful date. As the greatest of all translators of hymns, Neale helped to disprove his friend Benjamin Webb's words: 'I am more and more convinced that the age of hymns has passed'!

O come, O come, Emmanuel,
And ransom captive Israel.
That mourns in lonely exile here,
Until the Son of God appear.

Rejoice! Rejoice! Emmanuel
Shall come to thee, O Israel.

O come, thou Rod of Jesse, free
Thine own from Satan's tyranny;
From depths of hell thy people save,
And give them victory o'er the grave.

O come, thou Dayspring, come and cheer
Our spirits by thine advent here;
Disperse the gloomy clouds of night,
And death's dark shadows put to flight.

O come, thou Key of David, come,
And open wide our heavenly home;
Make safe the way that leads on high,
And close the path to misery.

O come, O come, thou Lord of Might,
Who to thy tribes, on Sinai's height,
In ancient times didst give the law
In cloud and majesty and awe.

From the Latin;
translated by John Mason Neale (1818–66)

Linda Berwick has worked for many years as a telephonist at an international bank in central London, and has also trained dozens of other girls at the job. She works in her local club for the disabled and has recently qualified as a psycho-therapeutic counsellor. She is herself severely handicapped – a spastic from birth and blind since teenage.

Linda has persevered against all the odds, through much painful surgery and despite official red tape. Her story has appeared in print and on television. She says that all the best things have happened to her since she lost her sight!

In 1975, she was confirmed at her church in east London by Trevor Huddleston, at that time Bishop of Stepney. The hymn she chose for that service was this simple prayer from medieval France. Linda usually reads the words of hymns from her own Braille copies kept in church. This one was short enough to memorize.

God be in my head,
And in my understanding.

God be in my eyes,
And in my looking.

God be in my mouth,
And in my speaking.

God be in my heart,
And in my thinking.

God be at my end,
And at my departing.

Anon. (Sarum Primer, 1558)

Thy Will Be Done, On Earth As It Is In Heaven

O Perfect Love

It was a Sunday evening in 1883. The Blomfield family was singing hymns round the piano at home in Ambleside in the English Lake District. At least one member of the family had her mind on other things: her wedding-day was getting very close. But what hymns should she have at the service? The words had to be just right – after all, she was a vicar's daughter!

Her sister Dorothy understood the problem. Quietly, she left the singers and went into the library with pencil and paper. Less than half an hour later, she came back with the draft of three new verses, beginning 'O perfect Love'.

The wedding took place, complete with its new hymn, which has since become the best known of all hymns about marriage.

O perfect Love, all human thought transcending,
  Lowly we kneel in prayer before thy throne,
That theirs may be the love which knows no ending
  Whom thou for evermore dost join in one.

O perfect Life, be thou their full assurance
  Of tender charity and steadfast faith,
Of patient hope, and quiet brave endurance,
  With childlike trust that fears nor pain nor death.

Grant them the joy which brightens earthly sorrow,
  Grant them the peace which calms all earthly strife;
And to life's day the glorious unknown morrow
  That dawns upon eternal love and life.

Dorothy Frances Gurney (1858–1932)

COURTESY OF WINCHESTER COLLEGE

Thomas Ken wrote these hymns for the boys of Winchester College. A pastor at heart, he disliked controversy. But he felt he had to cross swords with three successive kings of England on matters of principle.

While at Winchester, he refused to put his house at the disposal of Nell Gwyn, mistress of Charles II, during a royal visit. But Charles bore no malice; when the bishopric of Bath and Wells fell vacant, he said, 'Where is the little fellow who refused poor Nelly a lodging? Give it to him!'

Ken remained a loyal bishop under James II; but he resisted the monarch's increasingly illegal measures, to the point of being imprisoned in the Tower of London. And when William and Mary came to the throne, he could not in conscience take the Oath of Allegiance. Because he considered that his oath to the exiled James still held good, he was deprived of his position in the church and in public life.

AWAKE, MY SOUL

GLORY TO THEE, MY GOD, THIS NIGHT

Awake, my soul, and with the sun
Thy daily stage of duty run;
Shake off dull sloth, and early rise
To pay thy morning sacrifice.

Redeem thy misspent time that's past
And live this day as if thy last;
Improve thy talent with due care;
For the great Day thyself prepare.

Let all thy converse be sincere,
Thy conscience as the noon-day clear;
Think how all-seeing God thy ways
And all thy secret thoughts surveys.

Glory to thee who safe hast kept
And hast refreshed me whilst I slept.
Grant, God, when I from death shall wake,
I may of endless light partake.

Lord, I my vows to thee renew;
Scatter my sins as morning dew:
Guard my first springs of thought and will,
And with thyself my spirit fill.

Direct, control, suggest, this day
All I design, or do, or say;
That all my powers, with all their might,
In thy sole glory may unite.

Glory to thee, my God, this night
For all the blessings of the light;
Keep me, O keep me, King of kings,
Under thy own almighty wings.

Forgive me, Lord, for thy dear Son,
The ill that I this day have done,
That with the world, myself, and thee,
I, e'er I sleep, at peace may be.

Teach me to live, that I may dread
The grave as little as my bed;
Teach me to die, that so I may
Triumphing rise at the last day.

O may my soul on thee repose,
And with sweet sleep mine eyelids close –
Sleep that may me more vigorous make
To serve my God when I awake.

When in the night I sleepless lie,
My soul with heavenly thoughts supply;
Let no ill dreams disturb my rest,
No powers of darkness me molest.

O when shall I in endless day
For ever chase dark sleep away,
And endless praise with heaven's choir,
Incessant sing, and never tire?

Praise God from whom all blessings flow,
Praise him, all creatures here below;
Praise him above, ye heavenly host,
Praise Father, Son, and Holy Ghost.

Thomas Ken (1637–1711)

By 1950, the American writer Albert E. Bailey had made the Atlantic crossing by sea forty-nine times. And every Sunday on board, he says, this hymn was sung at the ship's morning service.

That is some measure of the pre-eminent place this holds as the 'sailors' hymn'. It is sung in war and peace, on great public occasions as well as by lifeboatmen or fishermen in lonely coastal villages – and now in many languages around the world too.

It is no surprise that Britain, a maritime nation, should produce such a hymn. The surprise is that it was left to a landsman to do it – a short, bespectacled schoolmaster whose health was never robust.

Eternal Father, strong to save,
Whose arm doth bind the restless wave,
Who bidd'st the mighty ocean deep
Its own appointed limits keep:
  O hear us when we cry to thee
  For those in peril on the sea.

O Christ, whose voice the waters heard
And hushed their raging at thy word,
Who walkedst on the foaming deep,
And calm amid the storm didst sleep:
  O hear us when we cry to thee
  For those in peril on the sea.

O Holy Spirit, who didst brood
Upon the waters dark and rude,
And bid their angry tumult cease,
And give, for wild confusion, peace:
  O hear us when we cry to thee
  For those in peril on the sea.

O Trinity of love and power,
Our brethren shield in danger's hour;
From rock and tempest, fire and foe,
Protect them wheresoe'er they go:
  Thus evermore shall rise to thee
  Glad hymns of praise from land and sea.

William Whiting (1825 – 78)

Frances Ridley Havergal was a natural musician and could have been a professional singer. She was not strong physically – she 'hoped the angels would have orders to let her alone a bit when she first got to heaven' – but she worked hard and used her musical and linguistic gifts to the full. This hymn was written on the last night of a five-day visit to a friend's home, where she wanted everyone to commit themselves wholeheartedly to God and experience his blessings.

She lived out the words in her hymns, too. She once wrote to another friend: '"Take my silver and my gold" now means shipping off all my ornaments – including a jewel cabinet which is really fit for a countess – to the Church Missionary Society...I retain only a brooch for daily wear, which is a memorial of my dear parents; also a locket ...I had no idea I had such a jeweller's shop...I don't think I need tell you I never packed a box with such pleasure.'

Take my life, and let it be
Consecrated, Lord, to thee;
Take my moments and my days,
Let them flow in ceaseless praise.

Take my hands, and let them move
At the impulse of thy love.
Take my feet, and let them be
Swift and beautiful for thee.

Take my voice, and let me sing
Always, only, for my King;
Take my lips, and let them be
Filled with messages from thee.

Take my silver and my gold;
Not a mite would I withhold;
Take my intellect, and use
Every power as thou shalt choose.

Take my will, and make it thine:
It shall be no longer mine.
Take my heart; it is thine own:
It shall be thy royal throne.

Take my love; my Lord, I pour
At thy feet its treasure-store.
Take myself, and I will be
Ever, only, all, for thee.

Frances Ridley Havergal (1836–79)

GIVE US THIS DAY
OUR DAILY BREAD

THANK YOU
FOR THE WORLD SO SWEET

Thank you for the world so sweet;
Thank you for the food we eat;
Thank you for the birds that sing;
Thank you, God, for everything!

Edith Leatham (1870–1939)

This hymn was written by a layman. The author of the original German words was in turn a Commissioner of Agriculture and Manufacture, a newspaper editor and a bank auditor. His Christian faith wavered under the influence of the eighteenth-century view that man was his own saviour and master of his own destiny. But after a serious illness he turned again to the Maker of all things, and the heavenly Father who loves and cares for his children.

He wrote this hymn as part of a dramatic sketch; its theme was the festival of harvest thanksgiving at a German farmhouse.

We plough the fields, and scatter
  The good seed on the land,
But it is fed and watered
  By God's almighty hand:
He sends the snow in winter,
  The warmth to swell the grain,
The breezes and the sunshine,
  And soft refreshing rain:
All good gifts around us
  Are sent from heaven above;
Then thank the Lord, O thank the Lord,
  For all his love.

He only is the maker
  Of all things near and far,
He paints the wayside flower,
  He lights the evening star.
The winds and waves obey him,
  By him the birds are fed;
Much more to us, his children,
  He gives our daily bread:

We thank thee, then, O Father,
  For all things bright and good,
The seed-time and the harvest,
  Our life, our health, our food:
Accept the gifts we offer
  For all thy love imparts,
And, what thou most desirest,
  Our humble, thankful hearts.

Matthias Claudius (1740–1815)
translated by Jane M. Campbell (1817–78)

'Either teach or learn, or leave': the motto, painted in Latin on the windows of St Paul's School in London, was hardly needed by John Milton, one of its brightest pupils.

He had 'a delicate, tuneable voice' and had inherited his father's love of music and books. He often sat up well after midnight to study Latin or Greek by candlelight. When he complained of headaches and tired eyes, no one recognized the warning signs; in his early forties he became totally blind.

Milton was fifteen, in his last year at St Paul's in 1623, when he wrote these lines. He put Psalm 136 into English verse, perhaps as a school exercise. This version makes him the youngest contributor to many hymn-books.

Let us, with a gladsome mind,
Praise the Lord, for he is kind:
For his mercies aye endure,
Ever faithful, ever sure.

Let us blaze his name abroad,
For of gods he is the God:

He with all-commanding might
Filled the new-made world with light:

Caused the golden-tressèd sun
All day long his course to run:

The hornèd moon to shine by night
'Mongst her spangled sisters bright:

He his chosen race did bless
In the wasteful wilderness:

He hath, with a piteous eye,
Looked upon our misery:

All things living he doth feed;
His full hand supplies their need:

Let us therefore warble forth
His great majesty and worth:

John Milton (1608–74)

Today we usually expect a service in church
to start with a hymn. But 200 years ago it was
different – only the psalms could be sung.

John Newton played an important part in
the battle to have hymns accepted in church.
While in Liverpool, he and his wife Mary
would often spend an hour on Sunday
evenings praying and singing with friends. In
his first parish as a minister, at Olney in
Buckinghamshire, the week-night meeting
where this hymn was first sung soon had to
move to larger premises. And on Sundays,
Newton's ministry attracted so many to the
services that a gallery had to be built in the
church to make room for everybody!

Glorious things of thee are spoken,
  Zion, city of our God;
He whose word cannot be broken
  Formed thee for his own abode.
On the Rock of ages founded,
  What can shake thy sure repose?
With salvation's walls surrounded,
  Thou may'st smile at all thy foes.

See! the streams of living waters,
  Springing from eternal love,
Well supply thy sons and daughters,
  And all fear of want remove.
Who can faint while such a river
  Ever flows their thirst to assuage?
Grace which, like the Lord the giver,
  Never fails from age to age.

Round each habitation hovering,
  See the cloud and fire appear
For a glory and a covering,
  Showing that the Lord is near.
Thus they march, the pillar leading,
  Light by night and shade by day;
Daily on the manna feeding
  Which he gives them when they pray.

Saviour, if of Zion's city
  I through grace a member am,
Let the world deride or pity,
  I will glory in thy name.
Fading is the worldling's pleasure,
  All his boasted pomp and show;
Solid joys and lasting treasure
  None but Zion's children know.

John Newton (1725–1807)

THE LORD'S MY SHEPHERD

A voyage from Britain to India in 1830 was nearly a disaster. A ship was wrecked in a violent storm off the Cape of Good Hope. No lives were lost, but almost everything else was. Alexander Duff, educational statesman and the first missionary sent to India by the Presbyterian Church of Scotland, lost an entire personal library – all except two books: his Bible and a Scottish Psalm Book were washed ashore. He took that as a parable. From now on he would concentrate on essentials.

In India, his household began each day by singing a psalm. And the words of Psalm 23 came vividly to his mind as he saw a shepherd leading his sheep across a precipitous track in the northern mountains. The man carried a long rod, with a hook at one end to help the sheep, and an iron band at the other for beating off wild animals. The rod and the staff, said Duff, were both needed – for guidance and defence.

This Scottish version of the twenty-third psalm is the consistent favourite among metrical psalms sung today.

The Lord's my shepherd, I'll not want;
  He makes me down to lie
In pastures green; he leadeth me
  The quiet waters by.

My soul he doth restore again,
  And me to walk doth make
Within the paths of righteousness,
  E'en for his own name's sake.

Yea, though I walk in death's dark vale,
  Yet will I fear none ill,
For thou art with me, and thy rod
  And staff me comfort still.

My table thou hast furnishèd
  In presence of my foes;
My head with oil thou dost anoint
  And my cup overflows.

Goodness and mercy all my life
  Shall surely follow me;
And in God's house for evermore
  My dwelling-place shall be.

Scottish Psalter (1650)

AND
FORGIVE US OUR TRESPASSES
AS WE FORGIVE THOSE
WHO TRESPASS AGAINST US

JESUS LOVES ME

In October 1949 Chairman Mao Tse Tung declared the establishment of the People's Republic of China. It quickly became apparent that all western Christians would have to leave the country. Soon mainland China was closed to Christians outside.

The church in China went through a very hard time. The little news that did leak out had to be discreet. And in one message received in 1972, there was a sentence which read, 'The *this I know* people are well.'

To the authorities the words did not make sense. But such is the international language of Christian songs that friends outside the bamboo curtain knew immediately that their fellow-believers were in good heart.

Jesus loves me, this I know,
For the Bible tells me so;
Little ones to him belong,
They are weak, but he is strong.

Jesus loves me! He who died
Heaven's gate to open wide;
He will wash away my sin,
Let his little child come in.

Yes, Jesus loves me; yes, Jesus loves me;
Yes, Jesus loves me, the Bible tells me so.

Anna Warner (1820–1915)

They brought Jesus to the place called Golgotha (which means The Place of the Skull). Then they offered him wine mixed with myrrh, but he did not take it. And they crucified him. Dividing up his clothes, they cast lots to see what each would get.

It was the third hour when they crucified him. The written notice of the charge against him read: THE KING OF THE JEWS. They crucified two robbers with him, one on his right and one on his left. Those who passed by hurled insults at him, shaking their heads and saying, 'So! You who are going to destroy the temple and build it in three days, come down from the cross and save yourself!'...

At the sixth hour darkness came over the whole land until the ninth hour. And at the ninth hour Jesus cried out in a loud voice, *'Eloi, Eloi, lama sabachthani?'* – which means, 'My God, my God, why have you forsaken me?'

When some of those standing near heard this, they said, 'Listen, he's calling Elijah.' One man ran, filled a sponge with wine vinegar, put it on a stick, and offered it to Jesus to drink. 'Leave him alone, now. Let's see if Elijah comes to take him down,' he said.

With a loud cry, Jesus breathed his last.

Mark 15:22-30, 33-37

When I survey the wondrous cross
  On which the Prince of glory died,
My richest gain I count but loss,
  And pour contempt on all my pride.

Forbid it, Lord, that I should boast
  Save in the death of Christ my God;
All the vain things that charm me most,
  I sacrifice them to his blood.

See from his head, his hands, his feet,
  Sorrow and love flow mingled down!
Did e'er such love and sorrow meet,
  Or thorns compose so rich a crown?

His dying crimson like a robe,
  Spreads o'er his body on the tree;
Then am I dead to all the globe,
  And all the globe is dead to me.

Were the whole realm of nature mine,
  That were a present far too small;
Love so amazing, so divine,
  Demands my soul, my life, my all.

Isaac Watts (1674–1748)

It was August 1756. A small group of people was meeting in a wooden barn in a village in Southern Ireland. The speaker, a layman named Morris, could hardly spell his own name, but he could read and understand the apostle Paul's words in Ephesians: 'But now in Christ Jesus ye who sometimes were far off are made nigh by the blood of Christ.' And, as he spoke, sixteen-year-old Augustus Toplady put his trust in Christ for the first time.

Toplady's most famous hymn grew from a single four-line verse appearing in *The Gospel Magazine.* He could be a bitter and obsessive controversialist, but this hymn has outlasted all his volumes of argument.

Rock of ages, cleft for me,
Let me hide myself in thee.
Let the water and the blood
From thy riven side which flowed
Be of sin the double cure,
Cleanse me from its guilt and power.

Not the labours of my hands
Can fulfil thy law's demands;
Could my zeal no respite know,
Could my tears for ever flow,
All for sin could not atone;
Thou must save, and thou alone.

Nothing in my hand I bring;
Simply to thy cross I cling;
Naked, come to thee for dress,
Helpless, look to thee for grace;
Foul, I to the fountain fly:
Wash me, Saviour, or I die!

While I draw this fleeting breath,
When my eyelids close in death;
When I soar through tracts unknown,
See thee on thy judgement throne,
Rock of ages, cleft for me,
Let me hide myself in thee.

Augustus Toplady (1740–78)

I AM THE WAY. THE TRUTH AND THE LIFE

A white-haired, hard-hitting Southern Baptist preacher called Mordecai Ham was leading an eleven-week evangelistic campaign in the town of Charlotte, South Carolina, in September 1934.

Among his crowd of listeners was a local farmer's son – tall, good-looking William Franklin Graham. He had not been too keen to attend – religion to him was 'all hogwash' – but this evangelist held him spellbound.

One night, as the choir sang 'Just as I am', the young man walked to the front, as a sign of his new-found faith in Christ, the Lamb of God.

Billy Graham has since become a world figure. He has spoken live to more people than any other man in history. And in every continent, in his own evangelistic crusades, he has used the hymn that meant so much to him.

> Just as I am – without one plea,
> But that thy blood was shed for me,
> And that thou bidst me come to thee,
>   O Lamb of God, I come.

> Just as I am – and waiting not
> To rid my soul of one dark blot,
> To thee, whose blood can cleanse each spot,
>   O Lamb of God, I come.

> Just as I am – though tossed about
> With many a conflict, many a doubt,
> Fightings and fears within, without –
>   O Lamb of God, I come.

> Just as I am – poor, wretched, blind;
> Sight, riches, healing of the mind,
> Yea, all I need, in thee to find –
>   O Lamb of God, I come.

> Just as I am – thou wilt receive,
> Wilt welcome, pardon, cleanse, relieve,
> Because thy promise I believe –
>   O Lamb of God, I come.

> Just as I am – thy love unknown
> Has broken every barrier down;
> Now to be thine, yea, thine alone –
>   O Lamb of God, I come.

> Just as I am – of that free love
> The breadth, length, depth and height to prove,
> Here for a season, then above –
>   O Lamb of God, I come.

Charlotte Elliott (1789–1871)

Mrs Alexander was the daughter of a major and the wife of a bishop. She was a tireless visitor, going from cottage to cottage in all weathers, supporting her husband's work in his diocese in Northern Ireland.

This hymn, dating from before her marriage, was written at the bedside of a child who was ill. The profits from *Hymns for Little Children,* where it first appeared in print, went to a school for deaf and dumb children in Londonderry. And Mendelssohn's friend William Horsley, who wrote the famous tune, was organist for eighteen years at a home for orphan girls in London.

The girl for whom the words were written recovered from her illness, and always regarded the hymn as especially hers, even when she grew up. Its greatness lies in the fact that so many other adults have done the same.

There is a green hill far away
  Outside a city wall,
Where the dear Lord was crucified,
  Who died to save us all.

We may not know, we cannot tell,
  What pains he had to bear,
But we believe it was for us
  He hung and suffered there.

He died that we might be forgiven,
  He died to make us good,
That we might go at last to heaven,
  Saved by his precious blood.

There was no other good enough
  To pay the price of sin;
He only could unlock the gate
  Of heaven, and let us in.

O dearly, dearly has he loved,
  And we must love him too,
And trust in his redeeming blood,
  And try his works to do.

Cecil Frances Alexander (1818–95)

When the Sabbath was over, Mary Magdalene, Mary the mother of James, and Salome bought spices so that they might go to anoint Jesus' body. Very early on the first day of the week, just after sunrise, they were on their way to the tomb and they asked each other, 'Who will roll the stone away from the entrance of the tomb?'

But when they looked up, they saw that the stone, which was very large, had been rolled away. As they entered the tomb, they saw a young man dressed in a white robe sitting on the right side, and they were alarmed.

'Don't be alarmed,' he said. 'You are looking for Jesus the Nazarene, who was crucified. He has risen! He is not here. See the place where they laid him. But go, tell his disciples and Peter, "He is going ahead of you into Galilee. There you will see him, just as he told you."'

Mark 16:1-7

Jesus Christ is risen today, Alleluia!
Our triumphant holy day, Alleluia!
Who did once upon the cross, Alleluia!
Suffer to redeem our loss; Alleluia!

Hymns of praise then let us sing, Alleluia!
Unto Christ our heavenly King, Alleluia!
Who endured the cross and grave, Alleluia!
Sinners to redeem and save; Alleluia!

But the pains, which he endured, Alleluia!
Our salvation have procured; Alleluia!
Now above the sky he's King, Alleluia!
Where the angels ever sing, Alleluia!

Anon. (Lyra Davidica, 1708)

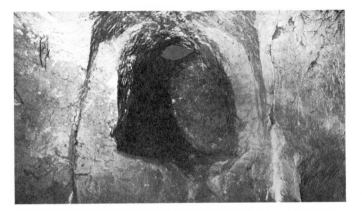

In spite of their differing temperaments, brothers John and Charles Wesley did many things together. At Oxford they formed the 'Holy Club' and earned the name of 'Methodist'; in Georgia they were none-too-successful missionaries; in London in 1738 they each found the experience that brought them peace with God. They also published hymn-books together. Although no one is quite sure which of the brothers wrote this hymn, Charles usually gets the credit.

He was converted to a living, personal faith while staying with a brazier called John Bray, who lived almost under the shadow of St Paul's Cathedral. On the Sunday when his 'chains fell off', Charles read in his *Book of Common Prayer* from Psalm 40: 'He hath put a new song in my mouth: even a thanksgiving unto our God.'

For the man who wrote nearly 7,000 new songs of praise to God, those were prophetic words.

And can it be that I should gain
   An interest in the Saviour's blood?
Died he for me, who caused his pain?
   For me, who him to death pursued?
Amazing love! how can it be
That thou, my God, shouldst die for me!

'Tis mystery all! The Immortal dies:
   Who can explore his strange design?
In vain the first-born seraph tries
   To sound the depths of love divine.
'Tis mercy all! let earth adore,
Let angel minds inquire no more.

He left his Father's throne above,
   So free, so infinite his grace,
Emptied himself of all but love,
   And bled for Adam's helpless race.
'Tis mercy all, immense and free;
For, O my God, it found out me!

Long my imprisoned spirit lay
   Fast bound in sin and nature's night;
Thine eye diffused a quickening ray –
   I woke, the dungeon flamed with light;
My chains fell off, my heart was free,
I rose, went forth, and followed thee.

No condemnation now I dread;
   Jesus, and all in him, is mine!
Alive in him, my living head,
   And clothed in righteousness divine,
Bold I approach the eternal throne,
And claim the crown, through Christ, my own.

Charles Wesley (1707–88)

And Lead Us Not Into Temptation, But Deliver Us From Evil

Guide Me, O Thou Great Jehovah

It was a fiery open-air sermon by Howell Harris, the Welsh evangelist, that gave to young medical student William Williams a new ambition and a new vocation.

And it was open-air preaching that Williams himself took up after an abortive start in the Church of England ministry. For almost half a century he travelled over the mountains, roads and tracks of Wales, averaging some 3,000 miles a year on horseback or on foot. Of the 800 hymns that he wrote in Welsh, this is his greatest. The tune 'Cwm Rhondda' did not appear until the twentieth century, but it is now inseparable from the words. And Welshmen are unrivalled singers of it, not least in the open air.

Guide me, O thou great Jehovah,
  Pilgrim through this barren land;
I am weak, but thou art mighty,
  Hold me with thy powerful hand:
    Bread of heaven,
Feed me till I want no more.

Open now the crystal fountain,
  Whence the healing stream doth flow;
Let the fire and cloudy pillar
  Lead me all my journey through:
    Strong Deliverer,
Be thou still my strength and shield.

When I tread the verge of Jordan,
  Bid my anxious fears subside;
Death of death, and hell's destruction,
  Land me safe on Canaan's side:
    Songs of praises
I will ever give to thee.

William Williams (1717–91)
translated by Peter Williams (1722–96)
and others

Martin Luther was the leading figure of the Reformation of the church in Germany in the sixteenth century. As an obscure monk studying at a university, he rediscovered for himself the teaching of the New Testament: the only way to God was through faith in Jesus Christ.

It was a time when ordinary people were being promised a way out of hell if they would give money to rebuild St Peter's Church in Rome. Luther spoke out against such abuses. He was keen that people should read and understand the Bible for themselves, so he translated the New Testament from Greek into German. He introduced the German language into church services, which had previously been conducted in Latin. Luther also led the way in congregational hymn-singing, setting new words to the popular tunes of the day. His aim was to 'sing the Reformation into the hearts of the people'.

A safe stronghold our God is still,
A trusty shield and weapon.
He'll help us clear from all the ill
That hath us now o'ertaken.
The ancient prince of hell
Hath risen with purpose fell;
Strong mail of craft and power
He weareth in this hour;
On earth is not his fellow.

With force of arms we nothing can;
Full soon were we down-ridden.
But for us fights the proper Man
Whom God himself hath bidden.
Ask ye, Who is this same?
Christ Jesus is his name,
The Lord Sabaoth's Son;
He, and no other one,
Shall conquer in the battle.

And were this world all devils o'er,
And watching to devour us.
We lay it not to heart so sore;
Not they can overpower us.
And let the prince of ill
Look grim as e'er he will,
He harms us not a whit;
For why? his doom is writ –
A word shall quickly slay him.

God's word, for all their craft and force,
One moment will not linger,
But, spite of hell, shall have its course;
'Tis written by his finger.
And though they take our life,
Goods, honour, children, wife,
Yet is their profit small;
These things shall vanish all;
The City of God remaineth.

Martin Luther (1483–1546)
translated by Thomas Carlyle (1795–1881)

WHO WOULD TRUE VALOUR SEE

Christiana and her four sons are nearing the goal of their pilgrimage when they meet a wounded man on the road. His name is Mr Valiant-for-Truth. They wash his wounds, give him food and drink, and learn his story as they travel on together.

Spurred on by the example of Christian himself, Mr Valiant-for-Truth had set out on the journey from the City of Destruction to the Celestial City. He relates the obstacles and battles along the way and, since pilgrims love to sing, launches into 'Who would true valour see...'

This is just a part of John Bunyan's masterpiece, *The Pilgrim's Progress,* an allegory of a Christian's spiritual pilgrimage. Now a classic of English literature, it was written while Bunyan was imprisoned in Bedford jail. He was persecuted for his faith and his preaching – but though his voice was silenced for a while, his pen was not.

Who would true valour see,
  Let him come hither;
One here will constant be,
  Come wind, come weather.
There's no discouragement
Shall make him once relent
His first avowed intent
  To be a pilgrim.

Who so beset him round
  With dismal stories,
Do but themselves confound;
  His strength the more is.
No lion can him fright,
He'll with a giant fight,
But he will have a right
  To be a pilgrim.

Hobgoblin nor foul fiend
  Can daunt his spirit;
He knows he at the end
  Shall life inherit.
Then fancies fly away;
He'll fear not what men say;
He'll labour night and day
  To be a pilgrim.

John Bunyan (1628–88)

Lead Us, Heavenly Father, Lead Us

If James Edmeston were to return to his native east London today – he was born at Wapping and died at Hackney – he would not easily recognize his surroundings. New housing estates and tower blocks have taken over where bombs fell or old buildings crumbled. It is even less likely that he would see many of the buildings which he, as an architect and surveyor, designed. However, the parish church of St Barnabas still stands in Homerton High Street. Edmeston was churchwarden there for many years.

This hymn, among 2,000 others he wrote, has outlived any of his environmental achievements and is now firmly established as a favourite choice at wedding services.

Lead us, heavenly Father, lead us
  O'er the world's tempestuous sea;
Guard us, guide us, keep us, feed us,
  For we have no help but thee;
Yet possessing every blessing
  If our God our Father be.

Saviour, breathe forgiveness o'er us,
  All our weakness thou dost know,
Thou didst tread this earth before us,
  Thou didst feel its keenest woe;
Son of Mary, lone and weary,
  Victor through this world didst go.

Spirit of our God, descending,
  Fill our hearts with heavenly joy,
Love with every passion blending,
  Pleasure that can never cloy:
Thus provided, pardoned, guided,
  Nothing can our peace destroy.

James Edmeston (1791–1867)

ABIDE WITH ME

At the FA Cup Final at Wembley Stadium in
April 1927, Cardiff City's 1-0 victory over
Arsenal took football's oldest trophy out of
England for the first and only time.

That match was also another 'first'.
King George V was one of the 100,000 crowd
who sang 'Abide with me' at a Wembley final
for the first time. And since 1927 the hymn
has always had a special link with Wembley.
These words are now heard every Cup Final
afternoon by a television audience of over 15
million in Britain alone, and by many more
millions on radio and television around the
world.

Abide with me; fast falls the eventide;
The darkness deepens; Lord, with me abide!
When other helpers fail, and comforts flee,
Help of the helpless, O abide with me.

Swift to its close ebbs out life's little day;
Earth's joys grow dim, its glories pass away;
Change and decay in all around I see;
O thou who changest not, abide with me.

I need thy presence every passing hour;
What but thy grace can foil the tempter's power?
Who like thyself my guide and stay can be?
Through cloud and sunshine, O abide with me.

I fear no foe with thee at hand to bless;
Ills have no weight, and tears no bitterness.
Where is death's sting? where, grave, thy victory?
I triumph still, if thou abide with me.

Hold thou thy cross before my closing eyes;
Shine through the gloom, and point me to the skies;
Heaven's morning breaks, and earth's vain shadows flee;
In life, in death, O Lord, abide with me!

Henry Francis Lyte (1793–1847)

The boys and girls at the Sunday School in the Yorkshire wool town of Horbury Bridge were the first people to sing 'Onward Christian soldiers', in 1864. Whit Monday was the day for the great processions of witness by the churches in many parts of the north of England and the children were due to join forces with others from a neighbouring village. They would march along, carrying banners, with the processional cross leading the way.

Their vicar, Sabine Baring-Gould, wanted something both rousing and new for the Sunday Schools to march to with real enthusiasm. So he stayed up all night writing, and in the morning produced the words of this, his most famous hymn.

Onward, Christian soldiers, marching as to war,
With the cross of Jesus going on before.
Christ, the royal Master, leads against the foe,
Forward into battle, see, his banners go.

Onward, Christian soldiers, marching as to war
With the cross of Jesus going on before.

At the name of Jesus Satan's host doth flee;
On, then, Christian soldiers, on to victory!
Hell's foundations quiver at the shout of praise:
Brothers, lift your voices: loud your anthems raise.

Like a mighty army moves the church of God,
Brothers, we are treading where the saints have trod,
We are not divided, all one body we –
One in hope and doctrine, one in charity.

Crowns and thrones may perish, kingdoms rise and wane;
But the church of Jesus constant will remain:
Gates of hell can never 'gainst that church prevail;
We have Christ's own promise, and that cannot fail.

Onward, then, ye people, join our happy throng;
Blend with ours your voices in the triumph-song;
Glory, praise and honour unto Christ the King,
This through countless ages men and angels sing.

Sabine Baring-Gould (1834–1924)

One Tuesday in March, 1858, 5,000 men were packed into the YMCA hall in Philadelphia. They listened to a young preacher, Dudley Tyng, preach on the text 'You that are men...serve the Lord'. The stirring sermon made a permanent impression on many of them. But it was Tyng's last.

A few days later, a tragic farm accident resulted in his right arm being amputated, and he never recovered from this severe shock. When he realized he was dying, he said to his father, 'Stand up for Jesus, father, stand up for Jesus. And tell my brethren of the ministry, wherever you meet them, to stand up for Jesus!'

The following Sunday, Tyng's friend and fellow-minister, George Duffield, read out in church this hymn which he had written, based on his friend's last sermon and dying message.

Stand up, stand up for Jesus,
  Ye soldiers of the cross;
Lift high his royal banner,
  It must not suffer loss.
From victory unto victory
  His army he shall lead,
Till every foe is vanquished
  And Christ is Lord indeed.

Stand up, stand up for Jesus;
  The trumpet-call obey;
Forth to the mighty conflict
  In this his glorious day!
Ye that are men now serve him
  Against unnumbered foes;
Let courage rise with danger
  And strength to strength oppose.

Stand up, stand up for Jesus;
  Stand in his strength alone:
The arm of flesh will fail you –
  Ye dare not trust your own.
Put on the Gospel armour,
  Each piece put on with prayer;
Where duty calls, or danger,
  Be never wanting there.

Stand up, stand up for Jesus;
  The strife will not be long:
This day the noise of battle,
  The next, the victor's song.
To him that overcometh
  A crown of life shall be;
He with the King of glory
  Shall reign eternally.

George Duffield (1818–88)

On the eve of Joseph Scriven's intended wedding-day, his bride-to-be was tragically drowned. Later he emigrated from Ireland to Canada. Once again he became engaged to be married, only to lose his second fiancée after a brief but fatal illness.

In spite of loneliness, poverty and his own precarious health, he spent the rest of his life helping the physically handicapped, as well as teaching and ministering among his fellow Christian Brethren in Ontario.

But it was not his own troubles that led him to write this hymn. He sent the words to his mother when she was going through a very distressing time. So, as with many other hymns, a private message has become a source of comfort to people across the world.

What a Friend we have in Jesus
  All our sins and griefs to bear;
What a privilege to carry
  Everything to God in prayer.
O what peace we often forfeit,
  O what needless pain we bear;
All because we do not carry
  Everything to God in prayer.

Have we trials and temptations?
  Is there trouble anywhere?
We should never be discouraged;
  Take it to the Lord in prayer.
Can we find a friend so faithful
  Who will all our sorrows share?
Jesus knows our every weakness;
  Take it to the Lord in prayer.

Are we weak and heavy-laden,
  Cumbered with a load of care?
Precious Saviour, still our refuge –
  Take it to the Lord in prayer.
Do thy friends despise, forsake thee?
  Take it to the Lord in prayer;
In his arms he'll take and shield thee,
  Thou wilt find a solace there.

Joseph Medlicott Scriven (1819–86)

Sarah Adams was the daughter of a radical political journalist who met his wife in Newgate Gaol, while serving a six-month sentence for defending the French Revolution. Sarah married a civil engineer, and her verses about Jacob's dream at Bethel became the favourite hymn of US President William McKinley, and of Queen Victoria and King Edward VII.

This hymn is also linked with the tragedy of the *Titanic,* the great ocean liner which sank on her maiden voyage across the Atlantic in 1912, with the loss of over 1,600 lives. As the ship began to tilt, Baptist minister John Harper asked the band to play 'Nearer, my God, to thee.' It was the last hymn in the lives of hundreds of people.

Nearer, my God, to thee,
  Nearer to thee!
E'en though it be a cross
  That raiseth me:
Still all my song would be,
'Nearer, my God, to thee,
  Nearer to thee!'

Though, like the wanderer,
  The sun gone down,
Darkness be over me,
  My rest a stone;
Yet in my dreams I'd be
Nearer, my God, to thee,
  Nearer to thee!

There let the way appear,
  Steps unto heaven;
All that thou send'st to me
  In mercy given:
Angels to beckon me
Nearer, my God, to thee,
  Nearer to thee!

Sarah Adams (1805–48)

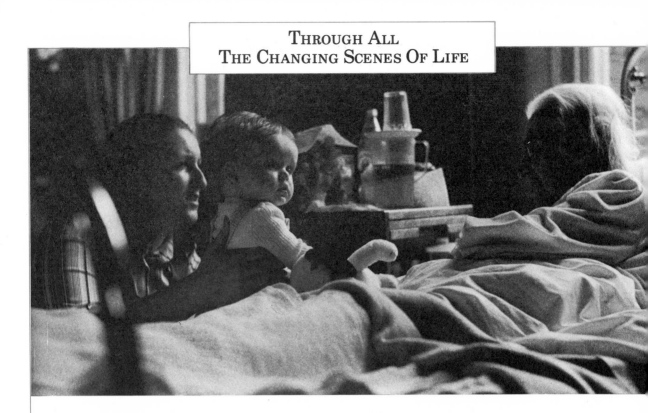

'Tate and Brady' were once as familiar and inseparable a pair of names as Laurel and Hardy or Rodgers and Hammerstein.

They were Irish Protestants whose *New Version* of metrical psalms, published in 1696, replaced the so-called *Old Version* of the previous generation. This version of part of Psalm 34 is the one survivor that has stayed the course for nearly three centuries.

But new versions always have their critics. Brady's own church would have none of it; to them it was 'an innovation not to be endured'. And Tate's brother had a maid who refused to come to family prayers because of it. 'As long as you sang Jesus Christ's psalms, I sung along with ye,' she said. 'But now that you sing psalms of your own invention, ye may sing by yourselves!'

Through all the changing scenes of life,
In trouble and in joy,
The praises of my God shall still
My heart and tongue employ.

O magnify the Lord with me,
With me exalt his name;
When in distress to him I called,
He to my rescue came.

The hosts of God encamp around
The dwellings of the just;
Deliverance he affords to all
Who on his succour trust.

O make but trial of his love,
Experience will decide
How blest they are, and only they,
Who in his truth confide.

Fear him, ye saints, and you will then
Have nothing else to fear;
Make you his service your delight,
Your wants shall be his care.

Nahum Tate (1652–1715)
Nicholas Brady (1659–1726)

For Thine Is The Kingdom, The Power, And The Glory, For Ever And Ever, Amen

For All The Saints

Sung to Vaughan Williams' majestic tune, these words convey a picture of great splendour. But their author was the humblest of men.

When he was a bishop in east London, William Walsham How refused to use a carriage, preferring to travel by public transport. He was known as 'the omnibus bishop' and 'the people's bishop'. He declined important posts in the church which in those days could have made him a rich man. His own son said that Bishop How lived a life which was itself 'a song of praise to his Creator'.

For all the saints who from their labours rest,
Who thee by faith before the world confessed,
Thy name, O Jesus, be for ever blessed:
Alleluia, Alleluia!

Thou wast their rock, their fortress, and their might;
Thou, Lord, their captain in the well-fought fight;
Thou in the darkness drear their one true light:

O may thy soldiers, faithful, true, and bold,
Fight as the saints who nobly fought of old,
And win, with them, the victor's crown of gold:

O blessed communion, fellowship divine!
We feebly struggle, they in glory shine;
Yet all are one in thee, for all are thine:

And when the strife is fierce, the warfare long,
Steals on the ear the distant triumph-song,
And hearts are brave again, and arms are strong:

The golden evening brightens in the west;
Soon, soon to faithful warriors comes their rest;
Sweet is the calm of Paradise the blessed:

From earth's wide bounds, from ocean's farthest coast,
Through gates of pearl streams in the countless host,
Singing to Father, Son, and Holy Ghost:

William Walsham How (1823–97)

LOVE DIVINE

Court composer Henry Purcell and Poet Laureate John Dryden were a powerful combination in late seventeenth-century England. When they got together to write a patriotic song – part of the opera *King Arthur* – it was an ideal partnership:

'Fairest Isle, all isles excelling,
Seat of pleasures and of loves,
Venus here will choose her dwelling
And forsake her Cyprian groves…'

But for Charles Wesley, a generation later, this was just not good enough. Venus, Jove and Cupid, he felt, were getting more than enough honours paid to them; so he wrote these new words to be sung to Purcell's tune.

Instead of pagan legends, Wesley's verses are full of the Bible; instead of glorifying the mythical deities of Mount Olympus, he wrote in praise of Jesus.

Love divine, all loves excelling,
  Joy of heaven, to earth come down!
Fix in us thy humble dwelling,
  All thy faithful mercies crown:
Jesu, thou art all compassion,
  Pure, unbounded love thou art;
Visit us with thy salvation,
  Enter every trembling heart.

Come, almighty to deliver,
  Let us all thy grace receive;
Suddenly return, and never,
  Never more thy temples leave:
Thee we would be always blessing,
  Serve thee as thy hosts above,
Pray, and praise thee, without ceasing,
  Glory in thy perfect love.

Finish then thy new creation,
  Pure and spotless let us be;
Let us see thy great salvation,
  Perfectly restored in thee;
Changed from glory into glory,
  Till in heaven we take our place,
Till we cast our crowns before thee,
  Lost in wonder, love, and praise!

Charles Wesley (1707–88)

ONCE, IN ROYAL DAVID'S CITY

For millions of radio listeners all over the world, Christmas begins with the clear treble voice of a Cambridge choirboy. Every year since 1919, this has been the opening hymn in the Service of Nine Lessons and Carols broadcast from King's College Chapel on Christmas Eve.

The hymn itself is much older than this particular service. It is one of the 1848 collection by Mrs Alexander, written to illustrate the words from the Apostles' Creed: '...born of the virgin Mary'.

Once, in royal David's city,
　　Stood a lowly cattle-shed,
Where a mother laid her baby
　　In a manger for his bed.
Mary was that mother mild,
Jesus Christ her little child.

He came down to earth from heaven,
　　Who is God and Lord of all;
And his shelter was a stable
　　And his cradle was a stall.
With the poor and mean and lowly
Lived on earth our Saviour holy.

And through all his wondrous childhood
　He would honour and obey,
Love, and watch the lowly maiden
　In whose gentle arms he lay.
Christian children all must be
Mild, obedient, good as he.

For he is our childhood's pattern;
　Day by day like us he grew.
He was little, weak, and helpless;
　Tears and smiles like us he knew:
And he feeleth for our sadness
And he shareth in our gladness.

And our eyes at last shall see him,
　Through his own redeeming love;
For that child so dear and gentle
　Is our Lord in heaven above:
And he leads his children on
To the place where he is gone.

Not in that poor lowly stable
　With the oxen standing by
We shall see him, but in heaven,
　Set at God's right hand on high,
When like stars his children crowned
All in white shall wait around.

Cecil Frances Alexander (1818–95)

JESUS LIVES!

The German Lutheran who wrote this hymn was known for his bad memory – and his generous spirit.

As assistant pastor to his father, he could not remember his own sermons well enough to preach without notes – and reading the sermon was frowned on. So he became a lecturer instead, and as Professor of Philosophy he filled his lecture-rooms to overflowing.

His kindness overflowed too. He gave away so much that when Prince Henry of Prussia visited him, he found him living in one empty room without food or fire. But, if only with this one Easter hymn, he has made many others rich.

Jesus lives! thy terrors now
   Can, O death, no more appal us;
Jesus lives! by this we know
   Thou, O grave, canst not enthral us. Alleluia!

Jesus lives! henceforth is death
   But the gate of life immortal;
This shall calm our trembling breath,
   When we pass its gloomy portal. Alleluia!

Jesus lives! for us he died;
   Then, alone, to Jesus living,
Pure in heart may we abide,
   Glory to our Saviour giving. Alleluia!

Jesus lives! our hearts know well
   Nought from us his love shall sever;
Life, nor death, nor powers of hell
   Tear us from his keeping ever. Alleluia!

Jesus lives! to him the throne
   Over all the world is given;
May we go where he is gone,
   Rest and reign with him in heaven. Alleluia!

Christian Gellert (1715–69)
translated by Frances Cox (1812–97)

In 1649, the reign of King Charles I of England came to a sudden and violent end – on the scaffold. But twenty-four years earlier it had begun splendidly enough, at a coronation service full of colourful pageantry and ceremonial. And one of the churchmen officiating then was John Cosin, later Bishop of Durham, who had produced a hymn specially for the great occasion.

It was a translation of a Latin work already some eight centuries old. Long before hymns became a regular part of church services in English, Cosin's version won its way as one of the only two hymns in the 1662 *Book of Common Prayer.*

Come, Holy Ghost, our souls inspire,
And lighten with celestial fire;
Thou the anointing Spirit art,
Who dost thy sevenfold gifts impart:

Thy blessèd unction from above
Is comfort, life, and fire of love;
Enable with perpetual light
The dullness of our blinded sight:

Anoint and cheer our soilèd face
With the abundance of thy grace:
Keep far our foes, give peace at home;
Where thou art guide no ill can come.

Teach us to know the Father, Son,
And thee, of Both, to be but One;
That through the ages all along
This may be our endless song,
   Praise to thy eternal merit,
   Father, Son, and Holy Spirit. Amen.

John Cosin (1594–1672)

By 1897 Queen Victoria had been Britain's sovereign for sixty years; no other English monarch had reigned so long. The Diamond Jubilee was celebrated in tens of thousands of churches – and centrally in London at Westminster Abbey. This hymn was specially chosen by the queen to be sung in every church on that occasion.

In the hymn-books it is usually found in the 'Evening' section; but John Ellerton wrote it, while a vicar in Crewe, for missionary meetings. Christians in the nineteenth century were becoming aware of their responsibility to take the gospel to the whole world, and this hymn clearly expresses their international vision. Even when Victoria's empire had crumbled away, the kingdom of Christ would remain.

The day thou gavest, Lord, is ended,
  The darkness falls at thy behest;
To thee our morning hymns ascended,
  Thy praise shall sanctify our rest.

We thank thee that thy Church unsleeping,
  While earth rolls onward into light,
Through all the world her watch is keeping,
  And rests not now by day or night.

As o'er each continent and island
  The dawn leads on another day,
The voice of prayer is never silent,
  Nor dies the strain of praise away.

The sun that bids us rest is waking
  Our brethren 'neath the western sky,
And hour by hour fresh lips are making
  Thy wondrous doings heard on high.

So be it, Lord; thy throne shall never,
  Like earth's proud empires, pass away;
Thy Kingdom stands, and grows for ever,
  Till all thy creatures own thy sway.

John Ellerton (1826–93)

Five-year-old Isaac Watts was asked by his father why he had giggled in the middle of their solemn family prayers. He said that through his fingers he had seen a mouse running up the bell-rope, and had suddenly thought,

'There was a mouse, for want of stairs,
Ran up a rope to say his prayers'!

But it wasn't until he was about twenty that he ventured to complain to his father about the grim verse of the metrical psalms they had to sing at Above Bar Chapel in Southampton. 'Try then whether you can yourself produce something better,' was the answer.

The young man who had learned Latin at four, Greek at nine, French at ten and Hebrew at thirteen, sat down to write straight away, and never looked back. In all, he wrote about 750 hymns.

Today, the chimes on the Town Hall clock at Southampton strike the notes, each quarter-hour, of the tune to which these words are now set.

O God, our help in ages past,
  Our hope for years to come,
Our shelter from the stormy blast,
  And our eternal home.

Under the shadow of thy throne
  Thy saints have dwelt secure;
Sufficient is thine arm alone,
  And our defence is sure.

Before the hills in order stood,
  Or earth received her frame,
From everlasting thou art God,
  To endless years the same.

A thousand ages in thy sight
  Are like an evening gone;
Short as the watch that ends the night
  Before the rising sun.

Time, like an ever-rolling stream,
  Bears all its sons away;
They fly forgotten, as a dream
  Dies at the opening day.

O God, our help in ages past,
  Our hope for years to come;
Be thou our guard while life shall last,
  And our eternal home.

Isaac Watts (1674–1748)

ALPHABETICAL INDEX OF HYMNS, WITH AUTHORS

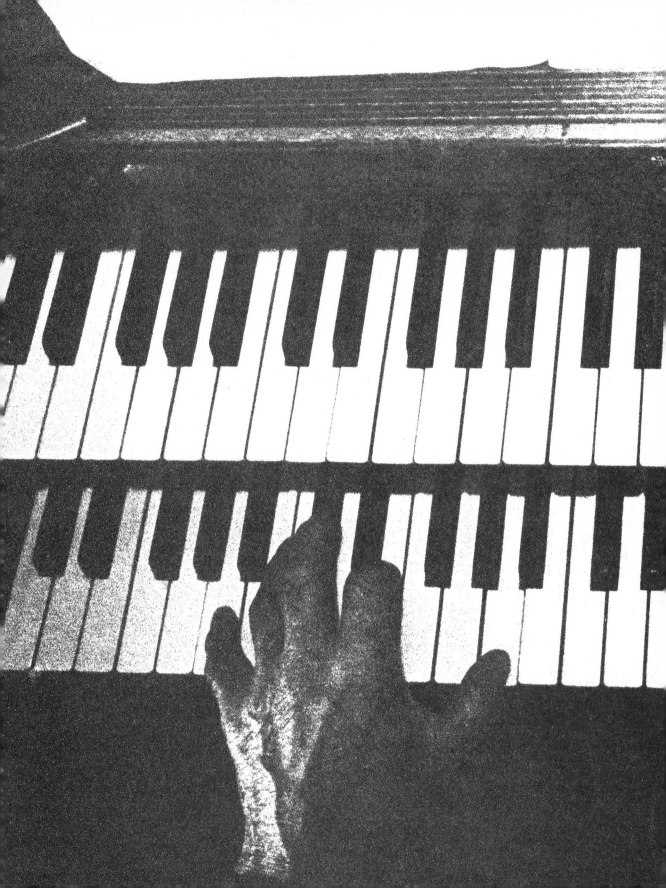